**THE SEASALTE**
**A SMUGGLING**

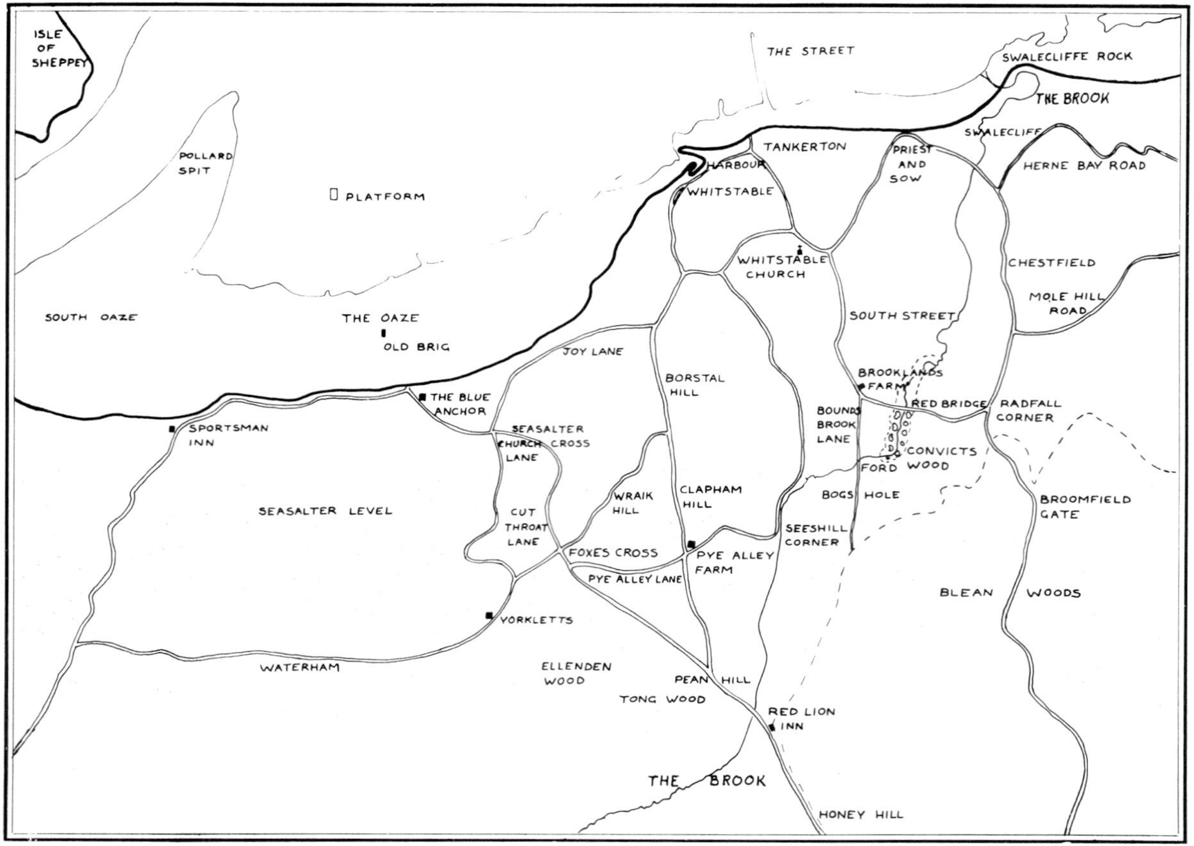
ISLE OF SHEPPEY
POLLARD SPIT
PLATFORM
SOUTH OAZE
THE OAZE
OLD BRIG
THE STREET
SWALECLIFFE ROCK
THE BROOK
SWALECLIFF
HERNE BAY ROAD
TANKERTON
HARBOUR
WHITSTABLE
PRIEST AND SOW
WHITSTABLE CHURCH
CHESTFIELD
MOLE HILL ROAD
SOUTH STREET
JOY LANE
BORSTAL HILL
BROOKLANDS FARM
RED BRIDGE
RADFALL CORNER
THE BLUE ANCHOR
SPORTSMAN INN
SEASALTER CHURCH LANE
CROSS
BOUNDS BROOK LANE
CONVICTS WOOD
FORD
SEASALTER LEVEL
CUT THROAT LANE
WRAIK HILL
CLAPHAM HILL
BOGS HOLE
BROOMFIELD GATE
SEESHILL CORNER
FOXES CROSS
PYE ALLEY FARM
PYE ALLEY LANE
BLEAN WOODS
YORKLETTS
WATERHAM
ELLENDEN WOOD
PEAN HILL
TONG WOOD
RED LION INN
THE BROOK
HONEY HILL

# The Seasalter Company - a Smuggling Fraternity
## (1740-1854)

by Wallace Harvey

*Books by the same author:*
Whitstable and the French Prisoners of War
Thomas Clark of Canterbury (1775–1859)

*First Printed*      *June 1983*
*Second Impression*    *June 1985*

© **WALLACE HARVEY**

All rights reserved. No part of this book
may be reproduced in any way without
permission from the publishers.

ISBN 0 9508564 1 X

Text set in Baskerville 11pt

*Printed and Published in Great Britain by*
*Emprint, 9 Harbour Street, Whitstable, Kent CT5 1AG*

## THE SEASALTER COMPANY

This innocent sounding title was used to designate the federation of a number of ostensibly quite respectable individuals, and to conceal the nature of their smuggling activities. Their business flourished for over one hundred years, during a time when that occupation was popular among all classes of people.

In order to understand and appreciate something of the working of the Company it is necessary to have an intimate knowledge of the history and geography of the countryside in which it operated. It is also useful to have some knowledge of the persons concerned. Even a casual amount of such knowledge will be sufficient to excite such relevant questions as, what was there at such an isolated place as Seasalter to attract and hold the interest of successive generations of important people who lived in such distant places as Ashford and Dover? What was there in such a desolate and lonely district to attract and induce such people to come and live there? Why should people, who were ostensibly strangers to the locality, want to invest their money in property there? What was there about this particular district, at that particular period that would induce people in a good station in life to seek to obtain obscure and poorly paid positions in the Customs service?

In an attempt to find answers to some of these questions it is first necessary to know that Seasalter is situated on the north Kent coast about seven miles east of Faversham and six miles north of Canterbury. During the period under review this particular part of the parish of Seasalter was only occupied by about five farms and a few small cottages. The low shelving seashore, fronted, when the tide ebbed, by extensive sand flats, and backed by acres of desolate marshes, provided an ideal coastline on which to land the contraband. Moreover the extensive forest of Blean, which stretched for miles in the hinterland, afforded ample and convenient places of concealment.

*Site of Thomas Patten's Parsonage*

There can be little doubt that during the period when the Company was active, the trade in contraband had become so well organised, that it was practically beyond the control of the Customs service.

The Rev. Thomas Patten, who was vicar of Seasalter from 1711 to 1764, lived in the vicarage which was then situated about two hundred yards from the seashore at the Blue Anchor corner, immediately on the east side of the road where the London to Whitstable railway now crosses it. He notoriously supplemented his living by smuggling. An interesting letter has survived which reveals one phase of his questionable activities. It was written from Canterbury on March 12th 1746 by Mr. Thomas Ketcherell, who was the Supervisor of the Eastern Division of Kent. It was written to Mr. John Collier, who was the surveyor General of the Riding Officers from 1733 to 1756, and is as follows.

"Dear Sir,
         I beg to acquaint you that on the 7th instant a gang of about one hundred and fifty smugglers landed their cargo between Reculver and Birchington and went from the sea

*The Blue Anchor*

coast about 9.0. a.m. Sixty three men and from eighty to ninety horses went by Whitstable and Faversham, and the rest went over Grove Ferry.

The Rev. Mr. Thomas Patten of Whitstable has let the Commissioners know when some gangs went through Whitstable for Faversham. It is reported that the Doctor formerly received tithe from some smugglers, but these gangs, being such rugged colts, (as the Doctor calls them), that nothing is to be got by them, made him angry."

This letter not only gives some impression of the size of the gangs engaged in smuggling at that time, and also of their method of operation, but it also emphasises how pitifully inadequate were the forces of law and order to combat the brazen activities of such large numbers of violent men. However, it is certain that while the big notorious gangs were successfully engaging the attentions of the Customs Officers, the members of the Seasalter Company were able to operate undetected and undeterred.

*Seasalter Cross*

The main object of the Company was to land the contraband at the Blue Anchor corner and to transport it by means of pack horses as quickly as possible to Blue House Farm at Lenham. This farm is situated in a quiet isolated spot, high on the hills to the north of the village, well back from the London to Ashford road, which runs along the bottom of the valley. This was used as the general clearing house for the contraband, a place to where the great transport wagons, going back to London from the coast, could, without raising suspicion, pull off the main road, rest the horses for the night, and load the desired quantity of goods without attracting too much attention.

Under the guise of keeping horses for rest and grazing on the Seasalter Marshes, large numbers of these animals were always arriving or leaving. This not only provided a ready excuse if suspicions were aroused, but it also ensured that large numbers of pack horses were always available when required to transport the contraband.

If it was not possible to quickly remove the incriminating

evidence from the locality, say for instance, by reason of the presence of the Customs or the Riding Officers, it then became necessary to disperse and conceal the contraband in a convenient place. Two such places so used were Seasalter Cross Farm and Pink Farm.

Seasalter Cross Farm, as its name implies, was situated adjoining the cross roads. Though it occupied such a prominent position it bore the reputation of having been used frequently as a place of concealment. Mr. Herbert Read, the aged grandson of Mr. Stephen Read, who was the farmer there in the days of smuggling, loved to describe his visits to his grandfather there, and with what relish his grandfather told stories of how the hay stacks would grow to twice their normal size in a night. The rich smell of tobacco on those occasions was an experience that he always remembered with pleasure. Then he would tell how a few days later, he would observe that the haystacks had reverted to their normal size.

Pink Farm, which stood at a short distance along Seasalter Lane, and was blessed with a spring of pure water, which never seemed to dry up, was at that time known as the "White House", because it was whitewashed in order to make it a conspicuous mark on a dark night, or when the marshes were shrouded in fog. However, in its later years it was coloured pink, hence its more modern name.

On either side of the great open fireplace was a large cupboard lined with shelves. The back of the cupboard on the righthand side was actually a door disguised by its shelves. When the house was demolished about 1953, this door was found to give access to a secret room about ten feet square. Disappointingly the room was found to be quite empty, with the exception of an old musket and a great pile of musket balls.

There were three bedrooms to the house. The centre bedroom, which was next to the great chimney, had no windows. In the dark corner behind the chimney was a kind of shaft about two feet square, with iron rungs across one corner. This shaft led down to the secret room. As there were no windows there was no risk of lights being seen from outside. The shaft provided an ideal means of passing food and drink down to anyone hiding there, or indeed a way of escape if the room was unfortunately discovered.

*Pink Farm*

Another story that has survived from those eventful days was told by an old man who likewise received it from his grandfather. It described how, as a boy, he was wont to take tea to his grandfather who was mowing reeds out in the marshes. On the way he had to pass a dry dyke, which to his amazement was filled with a great quantity of parcels. On reaching his destination he told his grandfather the exciting news, but to his astonishment it was received with absolute coolness. In fact the old man appeared to be quite unimpressed and not concerned in any way. He assured his grandson that he had most certainly been dreaming, and must imagine what he had seen. In fact he must be suffering from a touch of sunstroke, for he was absolutely sure that the dyke was quite empty. Strange to say the old fellow would not allow him to return by the same way that he had come, but sent him home along the seashore. The next day, the boy, still feeling very confused and mystified, went to see the dyke to prove that he had indeed been dreaming. Sure enough he found that the dyke was quite empty, and that was proof after all that his grandfather was quite right.

It was thought that the success of the "Company" would be seriously threatened just after April 26th 1831, when the Coast Blockade Stations, which had been manned by men from H.M.S. Ramillies, were taken over and manned by the Coastguards, under the control of the Coastguard Officer, Custom House, London. However it was soon found possible to come to an amicable arrangement suitable to all parties.

When a cargo was about to be landed under cover of darkness, Edward Gaskin, a strong young fellow, who possessed a loud voice, would furnish himself with a long plank of wood, and then station himself within hailing distance of the Coastguard Houses at Seasalter. On a given signal he would shout out such phrases as, "The coast is clear lads", "It's all right, come on", and, "There's no one about". This was the signal for the Coastguards to turn out and humourously pretend to chase him. With the aid of his long plank Gaskin was able to cross the dykes quickly and where he chose, in a direction away from the landing place. The Coastguards on their part took the slower way through the field gates. After an appropriate time had elapsed in the fruitless chase the Coastguards would return to their beds.

The next morning they were sure to find a barrel of brandy or a supply of plug tobacco accidently left on the beach.

By reason of the very secretive nature of the business our knowledge of the individual members of the Company must of necessity be based largely upon circumstantial evidence.

A revealing fact, and a connecting link in the chain of evidence is that, throughout the whole period when the Company was in operation, a prominent member either leased the Seasalter Parsonage Farm from the Dean and Chapter, or a member was always in residence there. There is no indication that Theophilas Hanly engaged in smuggling when he leased the farm about 1700.

From the knowledge gained from that source it would seem to be almost certain that the Company was founded by Dr. Isaac Rutton of Ashford, when he first leased the farm. He would appear to have been a most influential gentleman. His pedigree, going back to 1567, may be found set out in William Berry's "Pedigrees of the Families of the County of Kent", together with his coat of arms. From this source we learn that he was the son of Matthias Rutton of Ashford, Kent, who was born in 1681, and died in 1741. His mother was Sarah, daughter of Nicholas Toke of Godington. Isaac was born in 1711, and in 1743 he married Judith, daughter of Richard Stokes, of Caln in Wiltshire. He died in 1792, when his lease of Seasalter Parsonage Farm still had ten years to run.

The route followed by the Company's teams of Pack horses from the Blue Anchor Corner at Seasalter was via the marsh road past Pink Farm, through Yorkletts, Dargate, Herne Hill, and then by Brogdale Road, through White Hill, and on to Blue House Farm at Lenham. It is even in modern times a road little frequented, overlooked by only a few cottages.

In association with this route we find strong indications of the assistance Dr. Rutton probably received from his sons. Isaac Rutton, his eldest son lived at one time at Whitehill, and later moved to Chapel House, which still stands on the corner of Brogdale Road at its junction with the London Road, near Ospringe. Underneath Chapel House is the spacious crypt of the demolished St. Nicholas Chapel. This crypt of course offered a ready place of concealment when

*Seasalter Parsonage Farmhouse and Buildings in 1902*

danger threatened.

Writing about Chapel House Edward Hasted says, "About a quarter of a mile eastward of Ospringe Street is a good house called from the ancient oratory or chapel formerly adjoining to it, but pulled down within these few years, Chapel House. This oratory was dedicated to St. Nicholas, and was erected for a priest to say mass in, for the safety and good success of passengers, who left their acknowledgements for his pains in it. It belonged lately to Mr. John Simmons, who sold it to Isaac Rutton Esq., naming it Ospringe Place, in which he now resides."

Those who remember this elegant villa, as it was a few years ago, standing in its own beautiful grounds, must have very mixed feelings, and possibly experience some surprise, when they view the modern houses, totally different in their style of architecture, thickly clustering round the old house.

However, by living at Whitehill, and afterwards at Chapel House, Isaac Rutton junior was certainly in an advantageous position to assist his father in the prosecution of his secret business.

A similar strategical position was occupied by Dr. Rutton's second son, the Rev. Matthias Rutton, who, as vicar of Sheldwich, and rector of Baddlesmere and Leaveland, was well placed to give timely warning of the presence or the movements of any Customs Riding Officers.

If we were not in a position to appraise these facts it would be a complete mystery to account for the reason why an Ashford doctor should be interested in leasing the little known and remote Seasalter Parsonage Farm.

*Seasalter Parsonage Farm in 1983*

First Sale, May 12th, 1903.

# WHITSTABLE-ON-SEA.

## THE BOLINGBROKE ESTATE,

Situate a few minutes' walk of the Railway Station and Town, on high ground, IMMEDIATELY FACING THE SEA and having a long frontage to the Faversham Road. The Water Mains are laid in front of Estate.

Whitstable is the nearest seaside town to London on the Kentish Coast, one of the most healthy and is rapidly becoming one of the most popular holiday resorts. **Grand Views are obtained over the Bay. Sea Bathing, Boating, etc.** The purchase of land on this Estate is a sound investment of capital, and those who take the present opportunity of securing Plots will undoubtedly acquire an improving and remunerative property.

## Mr. J. BROOKE STEWART

Will offer for SALE BY PUBLIC AUCTION, in a Marquee on the Estate,
At 2.30 p.m on

### Tuesday, May 12th, 1903,

### 150 PLOTS

OF

## Freehold Building Land,

A VERY VALUABLE BLOCK, COMPRISING—

### SMALL FARM-HOUSE, BARNS and BUILDINGS,

ABUTTING ON THE MAIN ROAD; ALSO A

### VALUABLE HOTEL SITE & SEVERAL SHOP and MAIN ROAD PLOTS.

**TITHE FREE!   LAND TAX FREE!!   ROADS FREE!!!**
FREE CONVEYANCES.                    NO LAW COSTS.
*POSSESSION GIVEN ON PAYMENT OF TEN PER CENT. DEPOSIT.*

If desired, the balance may be paid by 9 Quarterly Payments. A Discount of Five per cent. will be allowed to all Purchasers who pay cash within one month of date of sale.

PLANS, PARTICULARS and CONDITIONS OF SALE may be obtained of the Vendor's Solicitors, Messrs. MAITLANDS, PECKHAM & Co., 17, Knightrider Street, E.C.; The Vendor, W. MARTIN, Esq., Derby House, Grove Vale, East Dulwich; and of the Auctioneer, Mr. J. BROOKE STEWART, 4, Fenchurch Buildings, E.C.

A Special Train leaves Holborn Viaduct Station at 11 a.m., calling at Elephant and Castle Station, at 11.3 a.m., Herne Hill 11.13 a.m., and Chatham 12.5. Returning from Whitstable at 7 p.m. A limited number of Free Railway Tickets will be issued, others can be purchased of the Auctioneer, at a charge of 4/- each, returnable to Purchaser.

### LUNCHEON FREE.

*Bill of Sale for Seasalter Parsonage Farm, 1903*

16

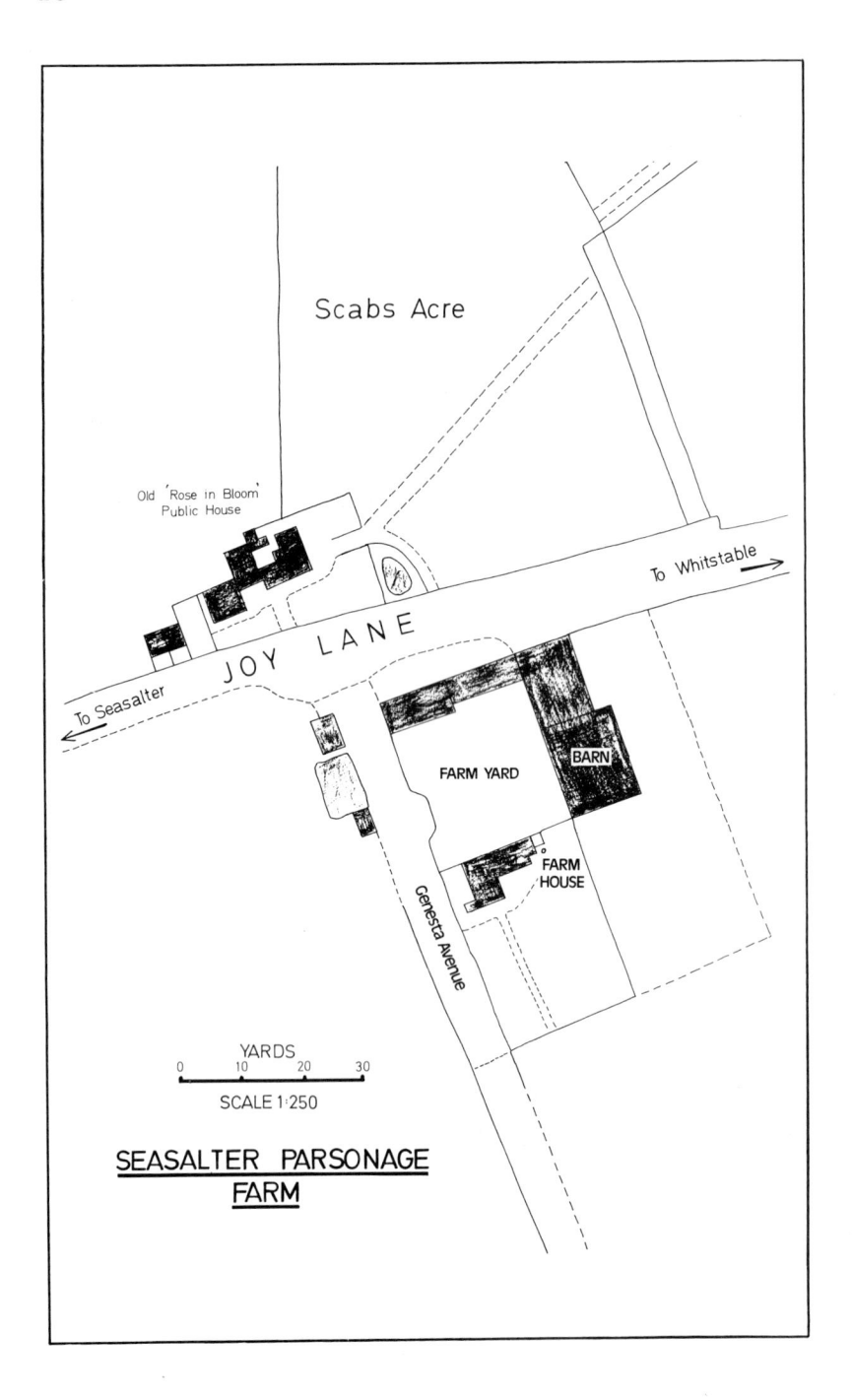

Scabs Acre

Old 'Rose in Bloom' Public House

To Whitstable

JOY LANE

To Seasalter

FARM YARD

BARN

Cenesta Avenue

FARM HOUSE

YARDS
0  10  20  30
SCALE 1:250

**SEASALTER PARSONAGE FARM**

Shortly after the death of their father in 1792, the two brothers assigned the lease of Seasalter Parsonage Farm to Mr. William Baldock, who lived in St. Georges Street, Canterbury, was a Justice of the Peace, and owned the brewery in St. Dunstans.

This event ushered in a time of great change in the conduct of the Company. Roads were being made up, and the age of horses and carts had arrived. The landing place for the contraband would now appear to have been moved to what was known as the Old Haven, which was situated just below the present Battery.

An old map of 1769 shows the roadway from the Old Haven, diagonally ascending the bank, just as it does now, and going straight to the Parsonage Farm. It was indeed an old haven, having been founded as the result of the destruction of the original landing place at the Blue Anchor Corner in the tidal surge of 1099.

We can only speculate on the reason for the mysterious accession of William Baldock to a position of wealth and power. There would appear to be little doubt that William Baldock started life in quite humble circumstances. Quite early in life he hired the Hoy Endeavour Inn, now 21-23 High Street, Whitstable, from Thomas Foord of Chestfield. This house was the headquarters for the lucrative business of smuggling the escaped French Prisoners of War back to France.[*] Baldock did not live at the house himself, but he installed Thomas Andrews as landlord. William Baldock on his part sailed a coasting vessel called the "Success", as the following advertisement from the Kentish Gazette informs us.

*May 1st 1776*
*NOTICE*
*W. Baldock*
*Informs the Public that his Hoy*
*the SUCCESS sails from Whitstable*
*every other Saturday as usual*
*and from the WOOL QUAY every*
*other Friday evening.*

It would be most interesting to know what Baldock did with his vessel during the intervals between his fortnightly sailings between Whitstable and London. We can only surmise

[*]*Available as a separate book entitled "Whitstable and the French Prisoners of War".*

that he made regular trips between the Old Haven and London, thus providing a much more rapid means of transport for the contraband than the old more dangerous route. However, what we do know is that his business prospered in a rapid and remarkable way.

From the Kentish Gazette only five months later we learn something of his prosperity.

> *September 11th 1776*
> *WILLIAM BALDOCK*
> *Hoyman from Whitstable to London. Begs leave to inform all the Gentlemen HOP DEALERS AND PLANTERS that he has now engaged TWO HOYS for the convenience of the London market during the season and intends sailing every week. He also has a large Storehouse at Whitstable very convenient for the storage of Hops. All other business will be transacted as usual with the greatest punctuality and every favour thankfully acknowledged by their most humble servant. Both his HOYS will sail this week. Canterbury, St. Georges Street. September 20th 1776.*

William Baldock indicated something of his deep involvement in the Free Trade when he took over the unexpired lease of Seasalter Parsonage Farm from Isaac and Matthias Rutton on the death of their father in 1792, but like his predecessor he did not live there. The men who were installed as tenants there all had strong connections with influential Dover families, and strongly support the suggestion that at this time the Company was actually managed from that port. The men thus installed here would appear to have acted as the local agents for the Company, they held positions of influence in the Customs Service, and employed their favoured office to conduct the business of the Company at the Seasalter end. They would all appear to have begun life in quite humble circumstances, then prospered to a remarkable degree, and ultimately retired to become important members of society.

Thus we find that when Dr. Rutton held the lease of Seasalter Parsonage Farm the man in charge there was John Knocker, a Dover man. He was described as Customs Waiter and Searcher at Whitstable. In the year 1782 his salary was £25 per annum, plus £15 to keep a horse. When he retired from Seasalter he was appointed Custom House Agent at Dover, and became Manager of the Bank at 17 Snargate Street.

John Knocker was followed at Seasalter by Thomas King, another Dover man, from whose marriage licence we learn the following particulars. "Thomas King of St. Mary Dover, Store Keeper to the Victualling Office at Dover, bachelor, and Elizabeth Causey of Dover, Spinster, 12th November 1766."

Twenty three years later we learn from the Kentish Gazette of July 14th 1789 that, "Saturday last Thomas King was appointed Tide Surveyor at Whitstable in room of Mr. J. Knocker."

After serving for two years at Seasalter he returned to Dover, set up as a builder, lived at No. 5 Chape Place, and was later appointed Deputy Registrar of Births, Deaths, and Marriages.

Eventually he bought Whitehall Farm, Shepherdswell, and retired there. Nevertheless he continued to take an active part in the affairs of the Company, and his will, dated 25th July 1815, reveals the extent of his substantial fortune.

Thomas King was followed at Seasalter by Edward Knocker who, when he retired to Dover, became a respectable Attorney-at-Law, and went to live in a house on Castle Hill. Much to his disgust his windows overlooked a filthy stretch of marshy ground, which was the site of an old tan-yard. He bought this piece of ground, and then, with the help of Thomas King as the builder, he built Castle Street across it, thereby not only cleaning it up, but also at the same time creating a profitable investment.

Later he purchased the large house of Mr. John Jeken, and eventually became the Town Clerk of Dover.

It is of interest to note that the legal transactions of the Company were conducted by Edward Knocker, the deeds being written and signed in his office.

Edward Knocker was followed at Seasalter by Thomas King's three sons and two sons-in-law, namely, John, Jonas, and Joseph King, and William Knocker, and Robert Walker. Each of these served the Company to the best of his ability and retired from Seasalter with every sign of being financially rewarded for their efforts.

Firstly, John King, who, when he retired to Dover, was described as a gentleman.

By far the most outstanding impression was made by his second son, Jonas King, who worked very closely with his father.

In the Custom records is preserved the following letter appointing Jonas King to his post at Whitstable.

*Ref. Customs /54/8. F.107.*
*Custom House,*
*Dover.*                                      *13th February 1794*

*Mr. Jonas King.*

*Dear Sirs,*
*Mr. Jonas King nominated to the office of Coastwaiter at Whitstable in the Port of Faversham having on perseverance to your Honours order of the 12th December last, No. 326, been instructed in the duties of the office of Coastwaiter and he appearing to be qualified for the said office, we respectfully transmit a Certificate thereof.*


*Custom House, Dover, 13th February 1794.*

*THE CERTIFICATE*

*This is to certify the Hon. Commissioners of His Majesty's Customs that Jonas King nominated to be a Coastwaiter at Whitstable in the Port of Faversham, who is to act as a Coastwaiter only and not to be employed in the original examination and delivery of Foreign Goods or Outwards hath in pursuance of the Boards Order of the 12th December last, No. 326, attended with the proper officers in this Port for the space of two months the lading and discharging and practice of Gauging and is properly qualified to execute the office of Coastwaiter in any part of this kingdom."*

Thus Jonas King was appointed as Riding Officer and Coastwaiter in 1794 at the princely salary of £25 per annum, plus £15 to keep a horse.

William Baldock had a brother Richard, and his Marriage Licence yields the following particulars.

"Richard Baldock of Elham, bachelor, and Mary Hobday of Barham, spinster, licensed to be married at Barham, 19th November 1771."

Richard was subsequently appointed Riding Officer and Coastwaiter at Herne in 1785 on the death of Henry Baker. From the land tax of 1796 we learn that he was a tenant of Gilbert Knowler at £3.

In the Kentish Gazette of August 4th 1795 we find a report of one of his exploits at that time, and the type of contraband smuggled. "On Tuesday last was seized between Faversham and Herne by Mr. Richard Baldock and another Officer of the Customs 13 casks of brandy."

Among other children born to Richard and Mary Baldock was a son named Richard Hobday Baldock, who was destined to follow in his father's profession. At present it has not been possible to find a record of when Richard sen. retired or died, but we find from the land tax that in 1800 he was still a tenant of Gilbert Knowler, and that his job had been taken over by his son at a salary of £33 per annum. In the Custom House records we find particulars of Richard Hobday Baldock's appointment as follows.

*R. H. Baldock, 23rd November 1799.*

*Custom House, Dover*  *Ref. Customs 54/P82*

*14th November 1799.*

*Dear Sirs,*
*In pursuance of your Honours order of 23rd of May last No. 101, we on the 14th September last past Mr. Richard Hobday Baldock nominated to be a Coast Waiter at Herne in the Port of Faversham under the care of the proper officers of this Port to be instructed in the business of that employment and he having taken copies of the forms of documents relating to the office of Coast Waiter, being conversant in the practice of gauging and appearing to us to be qualified for the*

*office to which he is nominated, we beg leave to enclose a certificate of the same."*

Thus Richard Hobday Baldock was duly sworn on the 23rd November 1799, and he was to receive a salary of £60 per annum.

Later in 1800 he received a further appointment to be Riding Officer, to ride Herne, Whitstable, and Reculver.

Without doubt he was in a favourable position to further the interests of the Seasalter Company by keeping a close watch on the activities of the other local smuggling gangs. Nevertheless he was compelled to live among a smuggling community and at the same time to be sociable and friendly with them.

Little effort was apparently made to conceal the activities of the powerful North Kent Company, which had its connections with the country surrounding Wingham and Littlebourne, and operated from Reculver whenever the tide was favourable regardless of the time of the day or night.

Nearer to the west, Baldock had the Thomas Hancock gang which operated from Bishopstone, and had its headquarters at Broomfield.

The Gayler Holness gang operated from Herne, and the Thomas Mount gang from Hampton. From the closely knit nature of the community of those days it would certainly be surprising if these smuggling gangs were not fully aware of his connection with the Seasalter Company, and it would not have paid him to make enemies of so many among whom he had to live.

Of course it was always possible for him to ride in the opposite direction and to see nothing. For some time at least his movements were well known when he was courting a young lady at Hoath. The marriage licence gives us the following particulars.

"Richard Hobday Baldock of Herne, Riding Officer, widower, and Susan Holtum of Hoath, spinster, 28, at Hoath, 9th October 1802."

Meanwhile Jonas King had undoubtedly found it profitable to be the local representative of the Seasalter Company, for during the next few years he was busily employed buying up houses and pieces of ground in all directions. As it transpired later he did not buy all this property with his own money.

If only the deeds of much of the property in this district could be inspected they would without doubt reveal a curious and frequent conveyance of the property between the individual members of the Company. From deeds already inspected it is evident that they frequently bought, sold, and re-bought the same properties among themselves every few months.

This practice no doubt provided a convenient screen for their financial operations, and at the same time ensured plenty of work for Messrs Knocker of Dover. Mr. Edward Knocker, Attorney-at-Law, with the assistance of his clerk, E. S. Williams, drew up the deeds, and thus ensured that the transactions would be private.

Three years after Jonas King had been appointed to Seasalter, and had come to live at Parsonage Farm, his father, then described as a builder of Dover, on the 31st May 1797, purchased the ground on which the Whitstable Public Library now stands. This piece of ground, not being sufficient for his purpose, he then bought the adjoining piece of ground from Robert Anderson, on September 4th 1797. On this prominent site Thomas King then built the largest and most imposing house in the town, complete with stables, coach house, and outbuildings. Then when this grand house was completed Jonas King moved there. At that time he was described as a Customs Waiter and Searcher, in receipt of a salary of £40 per annum. If we did not know we might well wonder how he could afford to live in such premises. This move made room for another member of the Company to live in the farm house.

Meanwhile the Free Trade continued to flourish all along this coast. The forces of law and order were pitifully inept, or reluctant to take any action in the matter.

The Kentish Gazette does indeed publish a few accounts of isolated captures made at this time by the Revenue Officers, but their very brevity leaves much to the imagination. Moreover there rarely appears to be a report of subsequent court proceedings or sentences. Thus we find on January 21st 1800 the following report.

"Tuesday was taken by Capt. Bread of the Queenborough Revenue Cutter, a large yawl with foreign spirits on board belonging to Whitstable."

How very interesting it would be if we could learn the name of the yawl and the names of the people involved.

The well known picture of the Lily Banks by J.M.W.Turner, 1826, showing the old road ascending the bank to Seasalter Parsonage Farm

25

*The same view as seen in the present day*

26

*The beginning of the Whitstable Public Library before the old house, (known as Oxford House), was demolished*

*The Whitstable Public Library in 1983*

Then just over a month later we have the following report.
"March 10th 1801.

Eleven half ankers of contraband spirits were seized by Revenue Officers in the parish of Seasalter on Thursday last, and on the following day at Whitstable, 37 half ankers, and some bags of tobacco."

This report gives a useful indication of the type of contraband that was being smuggled at that time, but of course no conception of the vast quantities that must have been landed without detection.

A piece of ground which played an important role in the operations of the Company was named Little Sea Field. It was described as being of nine acres, lying in the parishes of Whitstable and Seasalter. For some years it was owned by Thomas Sladden who, when he made his will on the 12th July 1727, left it to his grandson, Daniel Peake, who in his turn sold it to William Baldock.

Over the years it was let out at a very cheap rent to John Dyason, William Dawes, John Chambers, Thomas Andrews, William Ginder, and lastly to Jonas King, all of whom were known to be involved with Smuggling. Finally on February 25th 1799 William Baldock sold it to Jonas King, for £350.

Adjoining Seasalter Parsonage Farm on its eastern side was a useful farm called LITTLE JOY from which Joy Lane derives its name. This farm Daniel Peake sold on 30th April 1788 to Edward Foad for £300. It was described as, "A Messuage or Tenement now in two dwellings and 6½ acres of land." Some measure of the eagerness to obtain this property may be judged from the fact that Edward Foad sold it on 7th October 1801 to Jonas King for £850.

Whether it was this transaction that aroused the displeasure of the local community is not known, but they started to smash the windows of his house, as the following advertisement from the local papers informs us.

### Tuesday November 17th 1801

*Fifty Guineas Reward offered for the conviction of those who frequently broke the windows of Mr. King the Revenue Officer of Whitstable in the middle of the night, particularly on the previous nights of Friday and Saturday. Whosoever will give information to Mr. King of Whitstable or to Mr. Knocker*

*Attorney-at-Law of Dover, of the said offenders, so that they might be brought to justice, shall receive a reward of Fifty Guineas on their conviction.*

There is no knowledge that anyone was ever tempted by the offer of this reward to betray the offenders.

It is of interest to note that at the time of the census in 1801 that the population of Whitstable was recorded as being 1205, and that of Seasalter as being 419. Of this combined number of 1624, seventy eight persons were wealthy enough to qualify for votes, and as the united parishes were reputed to have fifty two public houses or beer houses, we have some indication of the strong local interest in the liquor trade.

Meanwhile the days of the transport by pack horses or asses were, or probably had already passed. The roads were being made up, turnpike roads were being constructed, and wagons and carts were being used for the transport of goods.

This of course exposed the smuggling fraternity to greater risk, especially when they were compelled to use the turnpike roads. Nevertheless it was a risk that it was still found profitable to take.

With the change in the method of transport the old long route to Blue House Farm at Lenham was discontinued, and the traffic was diverted to St. Dunstan's Brewery at Canterbury via Seasalter Cross, Church Lane, Cut Throat Lane, (now Pilgrims Lane) to Foxes Cross, and the main Turnpike Road at the top of Pean Hill. In the first instance William Baldock hired horses and carts from the local farmers to transport the contraband to his brewery, which in a way provided a respectable cloak for the real business.

Until recent years the route from the Blue Anchor or from the Old Haven to the top of Pean Hill was lonely and well screened by high banks, hedges, and trees. Even to well within living memory the thick Ellenden Woods extended right down to the roadway. From the top of Pean Hill and along the turnpike road to St. Dunstans there was always a very grave risk of being caught by the Revenue officers. However the people who lived along the road knew how to have a blind eye and to keep their mouths shut.

In order to provide an excuse for his activities in the locality, and also to have a convenient place where horses and carts could be kept ready for use, William Baldock proceeded

*Cut Throat Lane*

*Foxes Cross*

The house built by William Baldock in 1801

*Photo – Mr. W. M. Bishop, R.I.B.A.*

31

*The house built by William Baldock in 1801, viewed from the south in 1961.*

*Viewed from the north in 1983.*

to enclose a piece of ground on the west side of the top of Pean Hill, and thereon to build a house and stables.

Unfortunately for him, he had neglected to first obtain the permission of the Lord of the Manor of Whitstable.

Consequently he was ordered to appear in Court on Friday 13th October 1801. This for him would appear to have been both an unlucky date and day.

The charge was as follows.

"William Baldock hath lately inclosed a certain piece or parcel of land on part whereof he hath since erected two several Tenements or Cottages containing by estimation Forty Perches more or less lying and being in the parish of Whitstable aforesaid abutting to the King's Highway towards the East and North and to lands of John Baker Esquire and Tong Wood there towards the West and to a piece or parcel of land last mentioned towards the South, and that the said William Baldock hath lately inclosed a certain other piece or parcel of land containing by estimation Ten Perches more or less lying and being in or near Seasalter Lane in the parish of Whitstable abutting to the King's Highway towards the East and North and to Tong Wood towards the West."

Baldock contrived to be represented by a very able attorney in the person of Thomas Foord of Chestfield, who was also the head of the gang which smuggled the escaped French Prisoners of War back to France from Swalecliffe. Foord spoke eloquently on behalf of his client, humbly acknowledged his fault and offered his apologies. There was nothing else that he could do in the face of such an obvious fact. Perhaps by reason of the fact that Baldock was a prominent business man, a Justice of the Peace, and such an important person in the district, he was let off with a strong caution.

Baldock immediately proceeded to install Thomas Culver in the premises and to supply him with horses and carts.

As we view this house at the present time we may well meditate on the thrilling stories it could tell if only it could speak of those far off adventurous days when it was young.

There must have been a considerable amount of contraband passing through Whitstable at that time. On June 1st 1802 the Kentish Gazette reported that,

"On Sunday was seized at Whitstable, by the Supervisor and two Excise Officers, 264 tubs of foreign spirits, which were lodged in His Majesty's warehouse in this city."

We can only speculate on the enthusiasm with which modern newspaper reporters would have written about such an incident, how they would have described the thrilling capture of such a large amount of contraband, and the difficulty of transporting such a large quantity to Canterbury. Without doubt the smugglers of those days were far from lazy or weak, for each anker of brandy contained 8.226 gallons.

Shortly after the above event Thomas Culver was nearly caught in the act of transporting ankers of brandy from the Old Haven. The warning word was brought to him, just after the carts had passed Foxes Cross, that the Revenue men were on the way from Canterbury. It was then a question as to which party would arrive at Pean Hill first.

Culver flogged his horses along Seasalter Lane to the limit of their strength. Willing hands quickly unloaded the contraband and concealed it in Tong Wood, and Culver only just had time to get the sweating horses into the stable before the Customs Officers arrived, but he had no time to remove the carts from the roadway. Despite the very obvious signs of what had taken place, and every effort of the angry frustrated Excise Officers to make Culver confess, no real incriminating evidence could be found.

Some time later however the law did manage to regain some of its lost dignity when Thomas Culver appeared in Court on Monday 8th November 1802, to answer to the charge of, "Causing a nuisance in suffering his waggons and carts to stand in the King's Highway." The newspapers make no report of what his sentence was, but no doubt the fine was readily paid by his wealthy employer.

Three years passed and then for some reason it was decided to liquidate the Company. On June 29th 1804 the following advertisement appeared in the Kentish Gazette.

*TO BE SOLD*
*The Parsonage of Seasalter.*
*Consisting of a Messuage or*
*Tenement, barn, stable, outbuild-*
*ings, yard, garden, and several*
*pieces or parcels of glebe land*
*arable and pasture, thereunto be-*

*longing, containing by estimation 43 acres more or less, with the tythes of corn and hay of the Parish of Seasalter in the County of Kent.*

*The above estate is held by lease from the Dean and Chapter of Canterbury for 21 years commencing from Lady Day 1802. The Parish of Seasalter is a very fertile part of the County and consists of about 1,200 acres of land. Also all that piece or parcel of land called Little Sea Field containing by estimation, 9 acres more or less, situate lying or being in the parishes of Seasalter and Whitstable. Also all those six several pieces or parcels of rich Marsh land containing by estimation 42 acres more or less situate in the said parish of Seasalter and enclosed with a ring fence.*

*Also all that piece of rich arable land (late wood ground) containing by estimation 2 acres more or less in the parish of Seasalter aforesaid. Also a piece of arable land in Seasalter at a place called Little Joy, containing by estimation three acres more or less.*

*All the above premises are in the occupation of Mr. Jonas King. And also all those two Messuages or Tenements with the garden and appurtenances thereunto belonging, situate lying and being in the parish of Seasalter*

> *aforesaid and now in the occupation of William Parks and William Gambrill.*
> *The purchaser of the Parsonage will be expected to take the Maxhills, livestock, and husbandry utensils thereto at a fair apprisement. For further particulars of Mr. Knocker, Attorney-at-Law Dover, and of Mr. Jonas King at Seasalter. A map of the Parsonage and Glebe land may be seen at Mr. King's. Possession of the Parsonage and of the above estates, may be had at Michaelmas next.*

This advertisement gives us most valuable information regarding the extent of the property controlled by Jonas King at that time, and it would be most interesting to know the reason for the proposed sale. However William Baldock came to the rescue and within ten days of the advertisement appearing in the paper he contacted Thomas King and bought Jonas King's large house from him on July 10th 1804 for £800. This seems to have saved the Parsonage Farm from being sold for it was soon taken over by Thomas King's third son Joseph. After Joseph King had served his term at Seasalter he retired to Deal. He was then described as a merchant. It would certainly be of interest to know the nature of his merchandise.

Joseph was followed at the Parsonage Farm by Thomas King's first son-in-law, William Knocker, who was described in the deeds as a gentleman. Such indeed he appears to have been, for he served as Mayor of Dover in 1797, and again in 1802.

Then when William Knocker had retired from Seasalter he again served as Mayor of Dover in 1817 and 1832.

Finally Thomas King's second son-in-law, Robert Walker, came to serve his term at the Parsonage Farm, and appeared to prosper as his relatives had done. He was described as a brewer, and became the senior partner in the Dolphin Brewery, and served as Mayor of Dover in 1804 and again in 1818.

In the deed of conveyance of the large town house William Baldock is described as a gentleman of Canterbury, and Thomas King is described as a builder of Dover. It must have been very shortly after July 10th 1804 that Thomas King retired to Whitehall Farm, Shepherdswell, and Jonas went to live there also.

However William Baldock lost no time in moving his nephew, Richard Hobday Baldock, into the vacant house. Then the next year Richard was appointed as Riding Officer from Whitstable to Reculver and Coast Waiter at Herne, at a salary of £60 per annum. Within a few weeks something seems to have happened to make him fall from official favour. He was dismissed from his position and Henry Butcher was appointed in his place. However after a short time he appears to have been forgiven, and he was reappointed as Coast Waiter and Riding Officer at Whitstable, at a salary of £25 per annum, and £15 to keep a horse. If we did not know of his close connection with the Seasalter Company it would be something of a mystery as to how he managed to live in the large house on his reduced salary and eventually to buy Yorkletts Farm.

At some time during the next two years, William Baldock, not in the least daunted by his experience in 1802, proceeded to enclose another piece of ground on the east side of the top of Pean Hill, and thereon to build another house, barn, and stables.

As a consequence he was once again ordered to appear in the Court on Thursday 6th November 1806 to answer the charge of "Having newly erected a Messuage on the east side of Pean Hill, being as yet untenanted."

As had happened previously he was represented at Court by his able attorney, Thomas Foord, who as he had done before, humbly confessed the fault and pleaded for leniency. As no doubt he hoped, Baldock was let off with a strong warning and a caution not to do it again.

This house is still standing although the farm buildings have all disappeared.

Jonas King continued to live at Shepherdswell, and we next hear of him on 12th May 1810 when he had to sign a long document drawn up by Messrs Knocker, wherein he confessed that he had purchased Little Sea Field and Little Joy with money supplied by his father. He was then, by

*The house built by William Baldock in 1806 on the
east side of the road*

another lengthy document, compelled to convey these properties to his father. Apparently the matter had been brought to a head because Jonas King had sold to Stephen Perkins, of the parish of Seasalter, Yeoman, three and a half acres of the land of Little Joy.

It is quite possible that despite his considerable wealth Jonas King wanted more money at this particular time for he had bought or was in the process of buying Bybrook Farm near Ashford. Those who travel the road from Faversham to Ashford may still see the barn and grand house that he built at Kennington, now the Bybrook Inn, and wonder how a humble Customs Officer from Seasalter could make such a fortune.

William Baldock died on 21st December 1812, and by his will, dated October 30th 1812, he expressed his entire satisfaction with Richard, and he left the big house, and other property to "My dutiful nephew."

An interesting light is thrown on William Baldock by a report in the Observer, 21st December 1812, as follows.

*"A person by the name of Baldock, who died recently at Canterbury exhibited an instance of the accumulation of wealth from very small beginnings, in fact from nothing. He died at the age of a little more than sixty, possessed of one million and one hundred thousand pounds. He was originally a poor boy employed to look after cows, and remarkable for dirtiness and slovenliness. He afterwards carried the hod as a bricklayer's labourer, and at length, by dint of industry and parsimony, with some assistance, he amassed money enough to build the barracks at Canterbury, which he let to the Government at the rate of 6d. per week for each soldier, a practice which proved so profitable that in the course of a few years the whole building became his own, and continued to acquire wealth in various ways, till at the time of his death it amounted to the sum stated above."*

Those who read this extraordinary report and knew the truth must have given many a knowing wink and wry smile as they discussed it with their friends. This was an astounding amount of money to leave in any age, and if only the whole truth could be revealed it would certainly prove stranger than fiction.

After the death of his uncle, Richard Baldock would appear to have experienced a period of difficulty. Despite the fact that in 1815 his salary was raised to £80 per annum he continued to need more money. In 1818 he was compelled to supplement his income by having himself appointed as Coal Meter at Whitstable. This involved watching the colliers unload their cargo at the Horsebridge Whitstable, a rather monotonous and dirty occupation. His salary for this employment was paid by the Crown as follows:

|      |            |      |           |
|------|------------|------|-----------|
| 1818 | £22 - 16 - 7 | 1819 | £19 - 13 - 6 |
| 1820 | £25 - 10 - 5 | 1821 | £22 - 14 - 8 |
| 1822 | £22 - 13 - 9½ |      |           |

In 1820 Richard was apparently forgiven for his past faults and he was then re-appointed as the Principal Coast Officer of Riding Officers, although at the same salary.

Then when in 1822 his salary was again confirmed at £80 per annum he thereupon resigned his appointment as Coal Meter.

In a closely knit community, such as existed in Whitstable in the early 19th century, it naturally followed that everyone knew everyone. A hundred yards or so from Richard Baldock's house stood the house and workshop of Mr. James Adley, carpenter and builder. This house, until it was demolished in recent years, was known as No. 55 Oxford Street, and it was built by Mr. Adley in 1791 in view of his second marriage to Catherine Morris of Westbere, and it was here that his only son, John Adley, grew up to eventually become the Comptroller of His Majesty's Customs at Faversham.

It is therefore somewhat strange that there could have been any information about Richard Hobday Baldock and the local Customs Officers that he did not know. Yet he found it necessary to write the following letter demanding information.

*Custom House Faversham*
*8th September 1821.*

*Sirs,*

*We have an Order from the Honourable Board to make a return forthwith of the ages and length of service of the several Officers and Meters in the service of this Revenue, agreeable to the form on the back hereof and request you will fill up the same with your servitude and likewise the Coal Meters.*

*We are Sirs*
*Your Humble Servants*
*W. Coleman, Collector*
*John Adley, Comptroller.*

*P.S. We beg to have it returned as soon as possible and to include Mr. Greenland in the account, R. H. Baldock, Principal Coast Officer, Edward Hunt, Comptroller, Whitstable.*

To this Richard Baldock replied on 10th September 1821.

*OFFICE   NAMES   AGE   Number of years and total length of service*
*Principal*
*Coast Officer, R.H.Baldock, 48, Twenty One, Sworn 23rd November 1799, 21 years 9 months 18 days*
*Comptroller and*
*Coast Waiter, Edward Hunt, 50, Twenty Two, Sworn 2nd July 1799 22 years 2 months 8 days*

*Riding Officer, Thomas Greenland, 66, Thirty Three, Sworn 5th Jan. 1780, 33 years 8 months 5 days*

*Coal Meter, William Smith, 49, Nineteen, Sworn 20th December 1801, 19 years 8 months 21 days*

*Coal Meter, Thomas Reeves, 33, Six, Sworn 8th March 1815 6 years 6 months 2 days*

*Signed R. H. Baldock, Principal Coast Officer*
*E. Hunt, Comptroller.*

Sent 10th September 1821.

For years amusing stories were told of the smuggling exploits of two vessels both appropriately named the "FOX". Whatever the Customs Officers tried to do was always defeated by the age old excuse, "It wasn't me Sir, it must have been the other "Fox" ". Eventually in desperation the authorities ordered them to be held in any port where they could be found, and a proper description of them be recorded. The following letter was accordingly sent to Whitstable.

*Custom House, Faversham.*
*14th December 1821*

Gentlemen,

*We request to be informed which of the two vessels, (mentioned at the foot hereof) are now in being — one having been seized and taken to Dover. We think it may be necessary on your part to make the inquiry with caution or you may be foiled — see their papers if possible.*

*We are Gentlemen,*
*Your Humble Servants*
*W. Coleman, Collector*
*J. Adley, Comptroller.*

"FOX" R. Rigden, 12 71/94 tons. "FOX" Thomas Giles, 16 22/94 tons.

Baldock's reply to this letter was evasive and far from satisfactory and he was ordered to make a more minute examination of Thomas Giles' "FOX", with the following result.

*Coast Office, Whitstable.*
*26th December 1821*

Gentlemen,

*We received yours of the 14th instant and have endeavoured to see Rigden, which we could not till this morning, when he informed us his vessel, called the "FOX", was not at home as he had hired her out.*

*"FOX" Thomas Giles, 16 22/94 tons register. 16 14/94 Licence. 31 feet long, 11 7/12 feet broad. Valued £130.*

Your obedient and honourable servant,<br>R. H. Baldock.

*To the Collector and Comptroller, Faversham.*

There is no evidence that having devoted his Boxing Day to providing this information Baldock did any more to help Adley to solve the mystery. Knowing what we do of him we may presume that he shared with his local friends the amusement of teasing the Faversham Customs Officers.

We now come to the final phase of the Seasalter Company and the association with it of the Hyder family.

This connection may be traced back to Thomas Hyder, a seaman, who was a close friend of the vicar, the Rev. Thomas Patten. He married Elizabeth Dodd of Selling on 5th March 1729, and served as churchwarden of Seasalter in 1735—7, 1741—2, 1746—7 and 1748—9. His death and burial is not recorded in the parish register, and there may be some foundation for the tradition that he was lost at sea.

In 1759 his widow, who had been left with one son, born in 1745, married William Glover, who was described as a grazier and butcher of Seasalter. There are indications that William Glover's chief occupation was to provide grazing and keep for the pack horses which were required to transport the contraband.

It is of interest to know that one of the pieces of ground leased by William Glover was known as Hart's Field, and which abutted on to the east side of the modern Oxford Street, Whitstable, and stretched southward from No. 53 to Belmont Road.

When his mother married again young Thomas was only fourteen years old, but even at that impressionable age he had quickly learned the value of being involved in the profitable Free Trade, and in the manorial books he is recorded as enclosing a number of the pieces of waste land belonging to the Lord of the Manor of Whitstable, and on them to graze horses. The scattered nature of these pieces of ground, situated as they were all over the district, no doubt helped to conceal the real extent of his activities.

There is ample evidence however that even as a young man his business prospered, for he was quite early able to lease Downs Farm, where the Sir William Nottidge School is now situated, and also to hire some marshes adjoining Seasalter Cross from the Church for £4 per annum. Then when he had married Sybella Wells, a widow from Lympne, on the 3rd August 1778, he built a house for himself on Hart's Field. This house now forms the rear portion of No. 61 Oxford Street.

Most aptly Thomas Hyder named his house "Vepery Cottage" in allusion to the notorious exploits of the famous Indian soldier, Hyder Ali. It was in this house that his son William was born in 1787, and who was destined to become the last director of the Seasalter Company.

We learn from the Manorial Rolls that, like his father, he was enclosing pieces of waste ground in 1810, when he was twenty three. There is ample evidence that, like his father and step-father, he prospered in life, and in due time he married Sarah Eagleton of Belton Hall, Rutland, and they continued to live in Hawks Lane, Canterbury, until about 1839.

It has not been possible to ascertain the exact date when William Hyder joined the Company and took over Seasalter Parsonage Farm, Blue House Farm, and other land belonging to the Company. Although we know that the lease of the Parsonage Farm was renewed on Lady Day 1781, 1802, 1823, and 1844, there is no indication as to when he followed Robert Walker at Seasalter who was certainly back at Dover before 1818, when he was Mayor for the second time.

Although it appears that Thomas Hyder shared Downs Farm with Richard Baldock there does not appear to be any evidence that it was connected with the Company. When William Hyder took it over it was described as a "Messuage Farmhouse buildings and lands containing together in the whole 179a—3r—1p."

There can be little doubt that William Hyder prospered in his business transactions.

When the Court Lees Estate was advertised for sale on Friday June 26th 1795 it was described as, "Being desirably situated on an eminence adjoining the Turnpike Road from Canterbury to Whitstable and nearly an equal distance from both places." The estate was said to contain 214½ acres. William Hyder bought this desirable estate in 1818, and in the succeeding years he built the imposing mansion around the original house, as we see it today, but he did not go to live there until 1839. An interesting feature of his handiwork is the vast cellar which extends under the whole mansion. If only walls could speak they would no doubt tell us why the cellar was made so large and what type of merchandise was probably stored there.

William Hyder rose to be a director of the Whitstable to Canterbury Railway, a trustee of the Whitstable to Canterbury Turnpike Road, Deputy Lieutenant and Justice of the Peace for Kent, and an annual subscriber to the Kent and Canterbury Hospital from 1814 to 1856. When he died on 8th January 1858 his estate was found to contain over three thousand acres.

It would appear that Hyder had bought most of the property of the Company after he took control. This certainly applied to Blue House Farm. In his will it was described as, "A Messuage or Tenement, farm, and several pieces or parcels of land containing in the whole 90 acres situate at Lenham in the County of Kent in the occupation of Thomas Ballard." It is of interest to note that when Ballard voted in 1868 the farm was described as being in Otterden.

It may be some indication of the time when the Company ceased to operate when William Hyder sub-let the Seasalter Parsonage Farm to Henry Bing on 30th September 1854. The farm was then described as, "A Parsonage House, buildings, and lands containing together in the whole 52a—1r—35p."

Having mainly by the aid of old newspapers, old deeds, and traditional stories, established a mental picture of the part played by the gentry who, by means of their money and position, operated the Seasalter Company, there now remains the more difficult task of describing the equally important part played by the more humble classes of society.

Much has been written about the pitiful state of the labouring classes of those days, and the working people of this district were no exception to the rule. Poor and illiterate, they were very much tied to their masters. These were the people who risked their life, limb, and strength, to do the heavy lifting and the transporting of the contraband, and unless they were actually caught in the act of smuggling, and subsequently were hung or transported, they rarely attracted public notice.

It was the custom for the employers of those days to find their employees standing hopefully in Canterbury Market. They then bargained with both men and women to come and work for them and live in for as little as they could.

Fortunately for our subject, in 1962 some old farming accounts covering the years 1766 to 1829, were discovered among the papers pertaining to Honey Hill Farm, Blean.

Honey Hill Farm occupies a commanding position on the crest of the hill of that name, two and a half miles north of Canterbury, on the main road to Whitstable, and it has magnificent views towards the north and west over the well-wooded Denstroud valley.

*Honey Hill Farm House*

The date stone on the front of the house bears the inscription, M.B. 1683. This commemorates the fact that the red brick skin was built round the far older house by Ephraim Bedwell, a tanner of St. Dunstans, Canterbury, who married Mary Moat, widow of James Moat, in 1676. Thence forward successive generations of the Bedwell family continued to live there, and were deeply involved in the smuggling operations of both the Reynolds Gang, and the Seasalter Company.

After the two sons of Dr. Rutton had assigned the lease of Seasalter Parsonage Farm to William Baldock in 1792, the original route to Blue House Farm, Lenham, was discontinued, and the flow of contraband was diverted through Canterbury.

In order to understand and appreciate this change it is advisable to consult the sketch map.

The contraband was still landed at Seasalter, and then transported by horse and cart and hidden in Ellenden and Tong Woods until it was safe and convenient to transport it to its ultimate destination. To this end William Baldock leased a part of the extensive Ellenden Woods and also Tong Wood, and therein put a strong force of woodmen. From the old accounts we learn that their names were, Browning, Rock, Smith, Wraight, Dove, Bedwell, Saffery, Gull, Stupple, Hammond, and Anderson.

We have already seen that William Baldock was summoned to the Court for building a house at the top of Pean Hill without permission, in 1801, and that the occupant played an important part in the transport of the contraband from Seasalter.

This house also played an important part in the very efficient signalling system which was then operated, mainly it is affirmed by women. While it has not been possible to identify the houses that were involved at the Canterbury end of the line, we do have a firm tradition that the signals were sent on from Moat House, Blean, to Frogs Hall, from thence to Honey Hill Farm, and then to Baldock's House at the top of Pean Hill, then next to Clapham Hill Farm, and from thence to Martin Down Mill. From there the signal was sent to Borstal Farm, which stood where the present Fire Station is, and which belonged to the Reynold's family, and was used in the smuggling operations by that gang. From Borstal Farm the signal was sent to Sander's Farm in what is now Oxford Street, and so to Reynold's House, which stood at what is now the junction of Argyle Road and Oxford Street.

It was boasted that it was impossible for the Revenue men or the Dragoons to traverse the distance from the West Gate at Canterbury to St. Dunstans Church, before the message was received at Whitstable.

The method employed was quite simple to operate. A besom on a long rod was kept permanently in place in a chimney or a prominent tree. Then when danger threatened it was only necessary for the foot of the rod to be pushed into the fireplace or the foot of the tree to make the besom protrude into sight.

On receipt of the signal at Whitstable it was only necessary for the lady to stand in her front doorway, and repeatedly to pull her nose, and soon everyone was following her example.

If a cargo of contraband needed to be unloaded in the daytime then the signal given was to repeatedly raise and lower the besom. On the other hand if the operation took place at night then the message was sent by raising and lowering a light in a window. When however the message was received in the daytime, the good lady stood at her front door and repeatedly stroked her chin, with the result that soon everyone was spreading the warning to be extra alert and cautious.

When Mr. Bedwell received the message at Blean he would quickly inform his neighbouring farmers, and they in response would provide the necessary horses and carts and men.

Obviously there can be no record of the number so supplied but from the old records we may learn something of the capacity of the farmers when they combined to supply horses and carts and men to excavate gravel at Tyler Hill and cart it to patch up the side roads, which at that time were little better than cart tracks. Thus on February 19th 1827 we find recorded:

    2 carts, 1 day, Gibbs, 12/-.
    2 carts, 1 day, Fleet, 12/-.
    2 carts, 1 day, E. Bedwell, 12/-.
    1 cart, T. Bedwell.
    1 cart, Wotton.
    1 cart and three horses, Adley.

There is no indication of the number of men employed in this laborious work, but it is worthy of note that E. Bedwell carted 44 loads on that day, and Fleet carted 40.

We may safely infer from this that the men were evidently accustomed to hard work, and would always be available day or night for the transport of contraband.

After the contraband had been carted to Ellenden and Tong Woods it remained concealed there until it was transported to its final destination disguised as loads of faggots or loads of bark.

The economics of the woods as revealed by the old accounts easily arouse the suspicion that strange things were happening.

Having arrived at the appointed destination, and the valuable part of the load safely delivered, the faggots were then sold at ridiculous prices. Thus in 1819 faggots were sold for 8/6 per 100, or 3/6 for 50. We find things far worse in 1822 when 200 oak top faggots were sold for 1/3 per 100. There was no other mention made of payment for horses and carts and men.

There was also the mystery of the brisk trade in loads of bark. We can perhaps appreciate such entries as in 1819, "Two horses to Sandwich with bark, 9/6, or on June 29th 1824, "4 horses carrying bark to Faversham", because at both of those places there was a tannery, but unfortunately most of the entries do not give us that much information, and we are left to wonder what would private individuals be doing with loads of bark. For instance we may well question why loads of bark and faggots should be sent to Mr. William H. Baldock, of the Broadway, Petham. This was and is a little country village some six miles south of Canterbury. Hasted described it in 1800 as, "At the western boundaries it is covered with woodland." It is a temptation therefore to regard the following entries with suspicion.

1824
May 19th
    Load of timber to Petham for Baldock, £1 - 5 - 0.
May 28th
    Load of timber to Petham for Baldock, £1 - 0 - 0.
June 3rd
    3 horse loads of bark to Petham for Baldock £1 - 1 - 0.
    Carrying bark to Petham for Baldock 2 days, £2 - 10 - 0.

1825
May 21st
   3 horse loads of bark to Petham for Baldock, £1 - 0 - 0.
   450 poles from Tong Wood to Petham for Baldock, £1 - 0 - 0.
   It is quite easy to appreciate the reason for the following.
1826
December 19th
   100 bushels of sprats from Whitstable to Petham
   for Mr. Baldock, at 4d., £1 - 13 - 4.
   What inference however may we draw from the following entry?
1826
May 20th
   Load of beach from Stone Street to Whitstable £1 - 8 - 0.

   It is disappointing that most of the entries for the transport of faggots and bark do not mention any destination, and while the loads of faggots were sold for prices ranging from 1/3 to 8/6 per 100 there is no indication that any of the poor people who actually did the work ever received any reward for it.

   Mr. Richard Hobday Baldock, the Riding Officer, had Yorkletts Farm, which is adjacent to the western side of Ellenden Woods, and has commanding views over the Seasalter Marshes to the usual landing place, but he never saw anything suspicious.

\* \* \* \* \*

So from all these too sparse facts it is possible to build up a mental picture of a smuggling company which consisted of men who were apparently quite respectable, and who rose from humble origins to positions of importance and wealth. Moreover this Company managed to operate continuously from 1740 to 1854 without any serious clash with the forces of the Customs Service.

During recent years a great change has taken place in the district, housing development has transformed the face of the open farm land. Nevertheless it is still possible to tread in the wake of the smugglers and to view the far extending marshes, and to see many of the landmarks that were so familiar to our ancestors.